1/14

THE HUMAN
BODY IN 3D

THE EYE
IN 3D

rosen publishing's
rosen
central®

RUSTY HUDDLE AND
JENNIFER VIEGAS

Published in 2016 by The Rosen Publishing Group, Inc.
29 East 21st Street, New York, NY 10010

First Edition

Library of Congress Cataloging-in-Publication Data

Huddle, Rusty.
The eye in 3D/Rusty Huddle and Jennifer Viegas.—First edition.
     pages cm.—(The human body in 3D)
Audience: Grades 5 to 8.
Includes bibliographical references and index.
ISBN 978-1-4994-3589-4 (library bound) — ISBN 978-1-4994-3591-7 (pbk.) —
ISBN 978-1-4994-3592-4 (6-pack)
1. Eye—Juvenile literature. 2. Vision—Juvenile literature. I. Viegas, Jennifer. II. Title.
QP475.7.H83 2016
612.8'4—dc23

2015000237

Manufactured in the United States of America

CONTENTS

INTRODUCTION

The human eye—an amazingly intricate and small organ—provides people with the sense of sight. You use your eyes for so many different activities, from reading your textbooks and deciphering your teachers' work on smart boards to watching your favorite TV programs, texting messages on your cell phone, and discerning the various colors in a rainbow.

The eyes enable people to see where they are within their surroundings and help them to observe shapes and colors. When objects reflect or give off light, the eyes help to process the objects' images. Although the eye has numerous structures, including the orbit, iris, lens, pupil, cornea, aqueous humor, vitreous humor, retina, choroid, fovea, macula, and optic nerve, and parts such as receptors and nerves to help it process vision, the eye cannot work alone. Each eye must have signals and data transmitted to the brain for the actual information to be processed, stored, and then retrieved.

The eyeball measures about 1 inch (2.5 centimeters) in diameter (width). There are six muscles that attach to each eyeball and that control movement. The eyeballs and muscles contain blood vessels, nerves, and connective tissue. The lacrimal gland, inside the orbit, produces tears that wash over

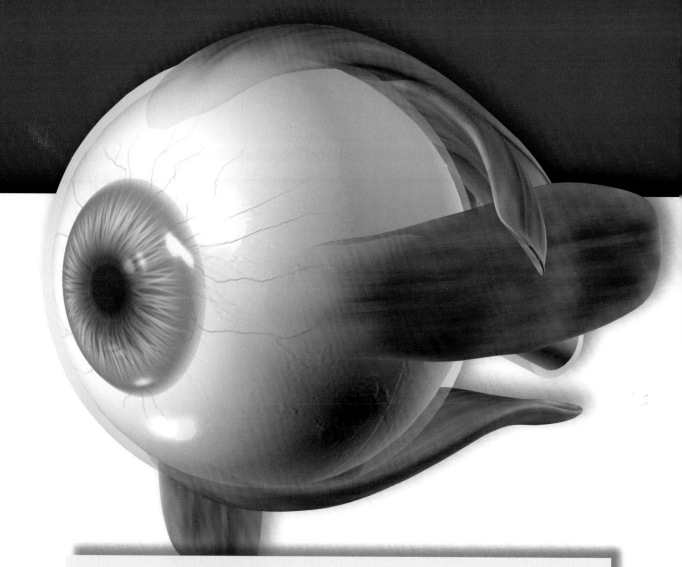

There are six muscles of the eye that control eye movement: superior rectus (top), superior oblique (top right), medial rectus (middle), inferior rectus (bottom right), lateral rectus (not shown), and inferior oblique (bottom).

the front surface of the eyeball and flow into sacs below the lower eyelid, draining into the nasal system of the nose. The eyelids contain special glands that give off oils to help lubricate the front structures of the eye, including the cornea. These structures and parts of the eye and their workings are explained here so that an overall picture emerges as to how vision takes place with help from the brain when all the parts are operating correctly.

As reported by the American Printing House for the Blind, there are approximately 60,393 students in the United States who are classified as being legally blind. The World Health Organization estimates that about 285 million people worldwide have some sort of visual disorder. Because of these high numbers, it is essential that people grasp the importance of good eye health and know how to determine the signs of the most common eye problems. The major causes of vision disorders are refractive errors, cataracts, and glaucoma.

According to some scholars, the ancient Greek philosopher Plato once said, "The eyes . . . are the windows of the soul." This resource offers an understanding of the eye's anatomy and its functioning. It also describes the workings of the visual system and some of the disorders and eye problems that are commonly encountered today. You'll examine the eyeball—external and internal structures—as well as aspects of color perception and measures of vision. Furthermore, you'll see in remarkable 3D photographs realistic views of how each part operates.

CHAPTER ONE

THE HUMAN EYE

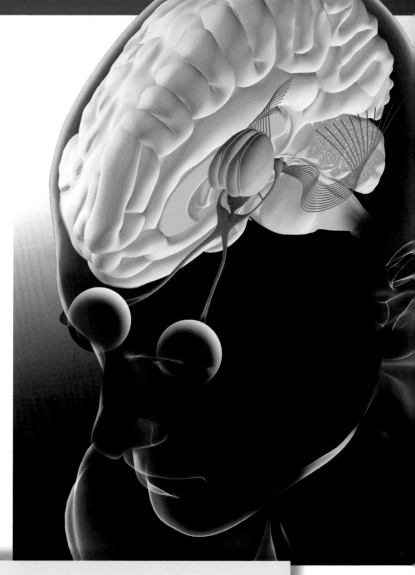

Humans rely on their sense of sight, also called vision, to move in their surroundings, and of the five senses (sight, hearing, smell, taste, and touch), it is probably the main sense used by most people. Because of the sense of sight, people's observed world has color, light, depth, shape, and movement. Vision is possible because of the structure and inner workings of

This representation of the right hemisphere (light gray) of the brain also shows the thalamus (light blue), the hypothalamus (dark blue), and the optic nerves (orange).

the eyes. Together with the brain, the eyes allow us to experience the vibrant shades of a rainbow or the subtle shadows cast under a moonlit sky. Stand in front of a mirror or, with permission, look into the eyes of someone nearby. Notice what appears to be a black dot in the center of each eye. This black circle, called the pupil, is actually a hole that reveals the darkness of the inner eye.

It is through this hole, and other parts of the eye, that light is able to enter from the outside world.

THE ORBIT

With your index finger, carefully touch the bony ridge underneath each eye. Following the contours of the bone, run your finger along its edges around the outside of the eye and toward the bridge of the nose. What you are feeling is the front section of the orbit, also sometimes referred to as the eye socket. This bone extends into the head and is shaped

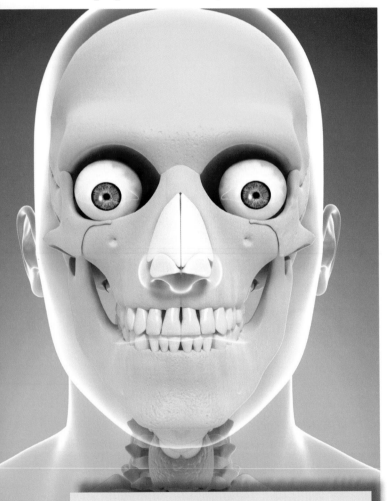

The orbits in the front of the skull are the two cavities that contain the eyeballs, eye muscles, fatty supporting layers, nerves, and blood vessels.

like a small salad bowl. The scooped curve in the middle helps to hold the eyeball in place.

As the word *eyeball* suggests, each eye is a round ball with an almost invisible bump at the front, the cornea. On average, eyeballs measure one inch (2.5 cm) in diameter. Muscles connected to the eyeball within the socket allow the eyes to swivel.

LINING THE EYELIDS AND EYEBALLS

The front of each eye appears to be shiny and smooth, almost like a thin layer of glass. That is because the eyes are covered with a transparent layer called the conjunctiva. The conjunctiva also lines the inner surface of the eyelids. The conjunctiva is a mucous membrane, or a thin, pliable section of tissue. The semiliquid mucus it secretes

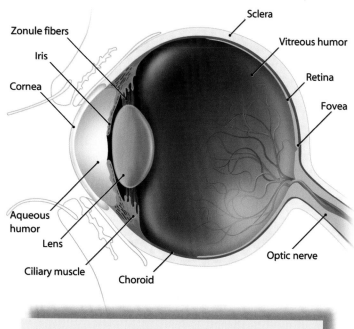

This diagram depicts the structures of the eye. The main layers are the protective outer layer (sclera and cornea), the middle layer (choroid, ciliary muscle, and iris), and the nerve inner layer (retina).

lubricates each eye, and, like window-washer fluid, helps to keep the eyes clean.

THE EYE'S WINDOW

The cornea serves as people's window to the world. Like a window, the cornea is clear and transparent so that light can travel through it. The cornea is shaped like a curved disk and is located at the front of the eye. It is able to focus on objects and gather visual information about them.

Seventy-five percent of the eye's power rests in the cornea, yet it is extremely small. At its center, each cornea is only about half a millimeter thick. At its sides near the sclera—the tough white part of the eye—each cornea becomes slightly thicker, but only by about another one-half millimeter.

Despite its very small size, each cornea consists of five different layers of tissue. The first layer, closest to the conjunctiva and the outside of the eye, is called the epithelium. It is like a very thin, clear sheet of skin. Next comes the Bowman's layer. It is made of sturdy, elastic material that gives the cornea flexibility. Underneath the Bowman's layer is the stromal layer. The stromal layer is the thickest section of the cornea. It consists of collagen, which is a tough, fibrous tissue also found in skin and bones. This layer contains antigens that produce antibodies. They help to keep the eyes free from infection.

The fourth layer of the cornea is called the endothelium. Unlike the stroma, the endothelium is quite thin, with the thickness of only one cell. It is extremely fragile and, once damaged, cannot heal itself. That is one reason why humans have protective eyelids. The endothelium helps to maintain water pressure in the eye and promotes transparency. The fifth and final layer is called the Descemet's membrane. It consists of a thin sheet of elastic tissue that, like the Bowman's layer, provides a certain amount of movement and flexibility to the cornea.

THE CLEAR FLUID CALLED THE AQUEOUS HUMOR

In anatomy, the word *humor* refers to bodily fluids. In this case, the aqueous humor is the clear fluid located behind the cornea. The chemical composition of the aqueous humor is somewhat like blood, but it does not have blood's high protein content. However, the fluid does contain nutrients, such as sugars and amino acids, to enrich the cornea and the front section of the eye.

The cornea is the transparent tissue at the front of the eye that is curved. The aqueous humor is the clear fluid that fills the eye's anterior, or front, chamber and posterior, or back, chamber.

Such nutrition is essential because the cornea itself does not have blood vessels. If it did, the cornea would lose its transparency.

The aqueous humor has two other important functions. It helps to keep the eye firm. By moving continuously, it also distributes nutrients and removes waste materials. The waste drains out through the canal of Schlemm, a channel that circles around the cornea. Tears perform a similar function. With each blink, the lacrimal glands above the upper eyelids wash antibacterial tears over the eyes to protect and clean them. Tears leave the eyes through ducts that drain through the nose. That is why you sometimes have to blow your nose after crying.

BEHIND THE AQUEOUS HUMOR

The iris and pupil are located behind the aqueous humor. As previously mentioned, the pupil is just a hole. The iris, the colored portion of the eye, determines how large this hole should be. Like strings opening a curtain on a stage, ciliary muscles pull the iris open and shut. When it is dark, the iris opens wide to permit more light to enter the eye. In bright sunlight, the iris closes up to protect the eye from too much light.

THE CRYSTALLINE LENS

Suspended within the eye, directly behind each pupil and iris, is the crystalline lens. Looking somewhat like a contact lens, this

HOW IS EYE COLOR DETERMINED?

Irises give each person a unique eye color. Some people have brown eyes, whereas others may have blue or green eyes. The color is inherited from their parents. Interestingly enough, only one pigment creates different color variations: melanin.

Melanin is the substance that gives skin, hair, and the irises a brown coloring. People with brown eyes have a lot of melanin and usually have darker skin and hair. Blue-eyed individuals, on the other hand, possess little melanin and often have lighter skin and hair. Green-eyed people have slightly more melanin but still tend to have lighter toned skin and hair.

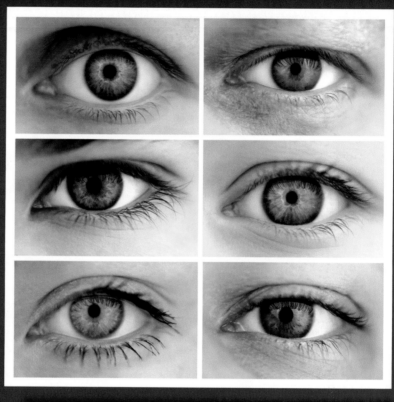

The iris is the colored, circular membrane that is suspended between the cornea and the lens. The iris's color depends on how much melanin is contained within its layers.

part of the eye can change shape to focus the light entering the eye, a process begun by the cornea. Stringlike ciliary muscles are attached to the top and bottom of the lens. When the muscles

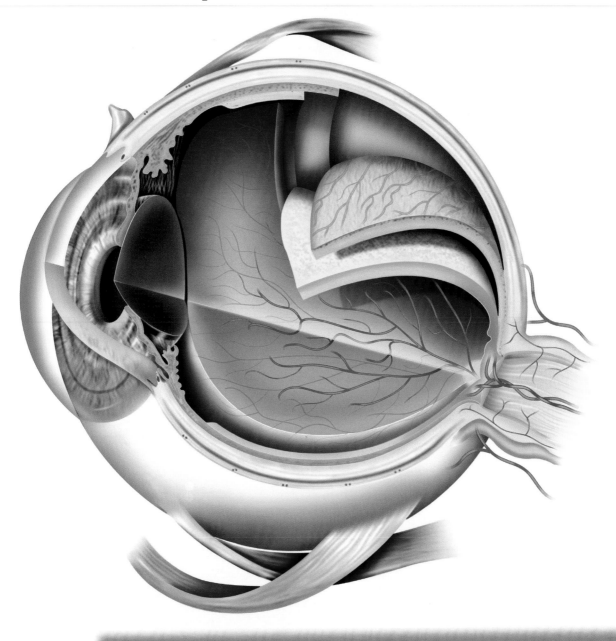

The inner nerve layer of the eyeball is called the retina (gold). It actually consists of several distinct cell layers, including the macula, where the area of clearest vision is located, and a light-sensitive photoreceptor layer of the rods and cones.

pull, the lens becomes more flat and narrow. This happens when we look at faraway objects.

Behind the lens is a substance known as the vitreous humor. It is a thick, white fluid that gives the eyes their firm, rubbery texture. Vitreous humor fills up most of the central chamber of each eye.

THE LAYER THAT LINES THE INSIDE OF THE EYEBALL

The inside of the eyeball, behind the vitreous humor, is lined with light-sensitive layers of cells. They form the retina, which serves as the film in the eye's camera. The retina contains two types of cells: rods and cones. Amazingly, each retina has 150 rods and 10 million cones.

Rods do not perceive color, but they work well in low light conditions. They are good at defining clear, sharp images. Cones do just the opposite. They detect color but provide little clarity when light is low. Most of the rods and cones are centered in an area of the retina at the inside back of the eye called the macula. The center of the macula contains an indentation, or depression, called the fovea. The macula and fovea help people to perceive fine detail in a process called central vision.

CHAPTER TWO

THE EYES WORKING WITH THE BRAIN

Although light and visual information are received through the eyes, they must be interpreted by the brain. Just as pixel data from a digital camera's sensor is sent to a computer chip for processing into images, images captured on the retina have to leave the eyes so that the pictures may be fully processed. What makes human sight better than even the most high-tech digital cameras is that the processing occurs in a split second, with most images simultaneously filed away for future reference

As images pass through a camera lens, they are turned upside down but then turned right-side up by the camera's software. When images are refracted to the back of the eye, they are upside down. Photoreceptors change them to impulses, which are sent to the brain by the optic nerve. The brain turns the images right-side up.

in people's memories. The eyes function similar to a camera while the brain handles all image development and processing. Nerves connect the eyes to the brain.

SENSORY NERVES CALLED OPTIC NERVES

Sensory nerves are bundles of special tissue that carry messages to and from the central nervous system, which consists of the brain and the spinal cord. Through chemical changes that create electrical impulses, nerves throughout the body can control everything from movement to sight. In a chain reaction, individual nerve cells, called neurons, pass electrical impulses to each other until the contained message reaches its destination. Like the plastic coating surrounding an electrical cord, a material called myelin forms a protective sheath around each nerve cell.

Tiny nerve fibers are connected to each of the retina's millions of rod and cone cells. These cells begin the chain reaction process by collecting information about objects, such as their size, shape, and color. The information in the cells transfers to the nerve fibers, which come together toward the back of the eye until they form the optic nerve.

This connection is similar to the electrical wires found at the back of most computer systems. Small wires join the basic components, while a larger cable connects the entire system to an outlet. The optic nerve functions like the computer's main

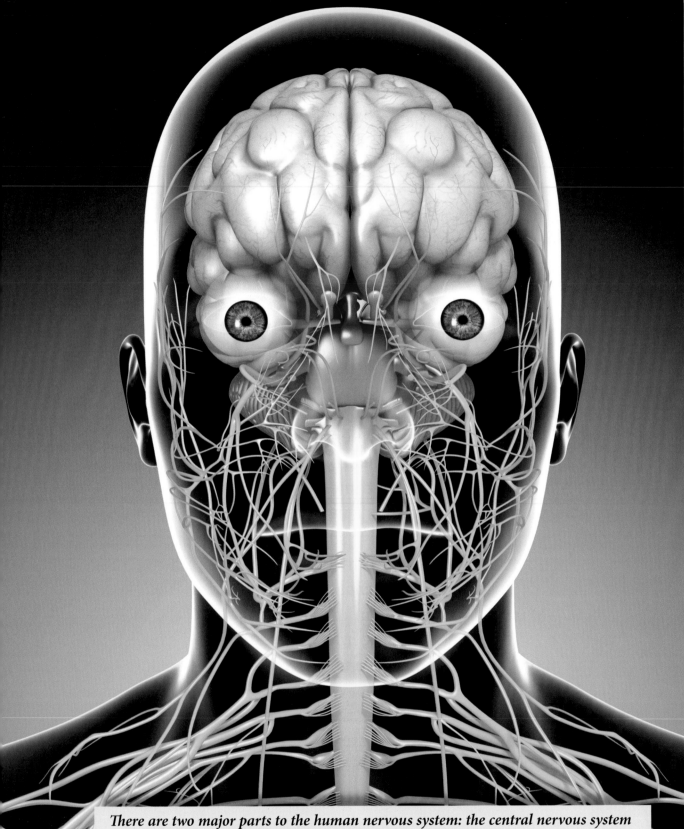

There are two major parts to the human nervous system: the central nervous system and the peripheral nervous system. The central nervous system consists of the brain, spinal cord, and optic nerves. The peripheral nervous system includes all the nerves that leave the brain and spinal cord and travel throughout the body.

cable. It gathers all of the nerve fibers from the retinas into two easy-to-manage bundles.

THE OPTIC DISK OR BLIND SPOT

The place in the retina where the optic nerve meets the back of the eye is called the optic disk. It corresponds to a natural blind spot because this area does not contain any light-sensing rods or cones. Since the eyes and brain usually compensate for the blocked view, people do not notice that anything is missing.

You can, however, find the blind spot for one eye by drawing 2-inch-high (5-centimeter-high) letters or shapes 3 inches (8 cm) apart on a straight line. Close the right eye and focus the left eye on the left object, holding the piece of paper at arm's length. Now, slowly bring the paper close to your face. The right object seems to disappear!

The optic disk does not contain photoreceptor cells (rods and cones) and therefore cannot perceive images. This spot is where the retina's cells collect, become the optic nerve, and leave the back of the eyeball.

19

THE CHOROID AND SUPPLYING BLOOD AND NUTRIENTS

A layer in the eye just above the retina, called the choroid, helps to maintain and feed the retina. Nutrients and oxygen are able to reach the retina through a network of blood vessels in the choroid. Arteries bring in nourishment, while veins carry out waste products.

Just as small nerve fibers gather to form the optic nerve, the arteries and veins merge into larger blood vessels that serve the optic nerve. The main artery that delivers blood to the optic nerve is called the central retinal artery. It runs down the middle of the entire optic nerve. The central retinal vein corresponds to this artery and helps to drain waste material and fluid out of the retina.

THE X-SHAPED STRUCTURE CALLED THE OPTIC CHIASMA

Place a hand over your right eye. Pay attention to what your left eye can see. Now place a hand over your left eye, and make a mental note of what is visible. As you probably noticed, each eye has a slightly different view. Yet despite the two eyes and these two differing views, people have just one field of vision. This field of vision is made possible, in part, because of the transfer of information that takes place at the X-shaped structure called the optic chiasma.

Optic nerves running from the left and right eyes merge and cross to form the optic chiasma in the brain, near the pituitary gland. Here, some of the data collected by rods and cones in the right eye is mixed with information collected by the rods and cones in the left eye.

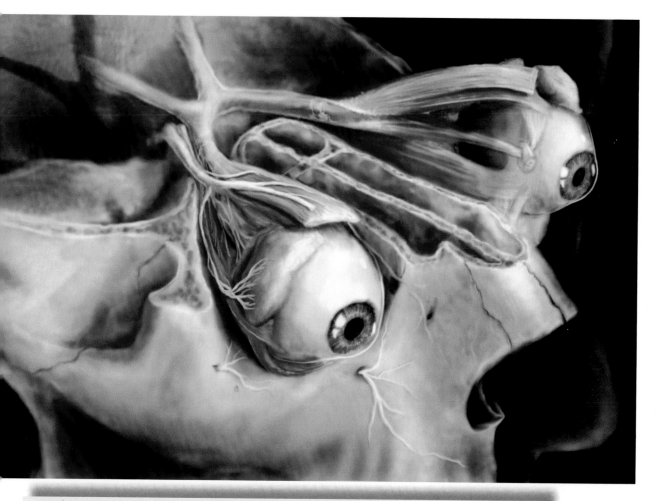

At the optic chiasma, nerve fibers coming from each eye split off from their optic nerves and cross over to the opposite side. Fibers containing information about the right visual field are on the left side of the brain, and those about the left visual field are on the right side.

A RELAY STATION CALLED THE LATERAL GENICULATE BODY

After the optic chiasma crossover, the two optic nerves fan out again in the brain. They then curve inward and meet at a place called the lateral geniculate body, which serves as a sort of relay station for visual information from the retina to the brain. The lateral geniculate body, which is also called the lateral geniculate nucleus, looks like two small balloons stuck together on top of three tiny eggs and is located in the thalamus of the brain. As at the optic chiasma, the optic nerves exchange information at the lateral geniculate body. There the brain analyzes how the two pupils react to observed light levels.

THE FANLIKE PATHWAY CALLED OPTIC RADIATION

After leaving the lateral geniculate body, the optic nerves fan out yet again, forming a heart shape around the parts of the brain called the temporal lobes. The temporal lobes handle hearing and smell, so the optic nerves take a detour around this section. The heart-shaped path that they take is called the optic radiation because *radiate* means to spread out.

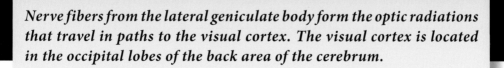

Nerve fibers from the lateral geniculate body form the optic radiations that travel in paths to the visual cortex. The visual cortex is located in the occipital lobes of the back area of the cerebrum.

THE STRUCTURE CALLED THE INTERNAL CAPSULE

Near the bottom of the heart shape where the two optic nerves meet is the internal capsule. It is the last point of exchange before information collected by the optic nerves heads into the final processing stage in the brain. The internal capsule houses most of the body's data concerning movement and the senses. Here, other nerves pick up information about spatial awareness and memory from the optic nerves. This data is sent to the prefrontal lobes, which are areas in the brain that specialize in depth perception and memory.

SENSORY AREAS CALLED THE PRIMARY AND SECONDARY VISUAL CORTICES

The nerve signals traveling along the optic nerve finish their journey at the back of the brain in the area of the visual cortices. The primary visual cortex is located at the very back of the brain and head. The secondary visual cortex is directly in front of it. To get an idea of where these are located, take a hand and run it up the back of your neck and across the back of the head. Where the skull slightly bulges out is approximately where the visual cortices are, about an

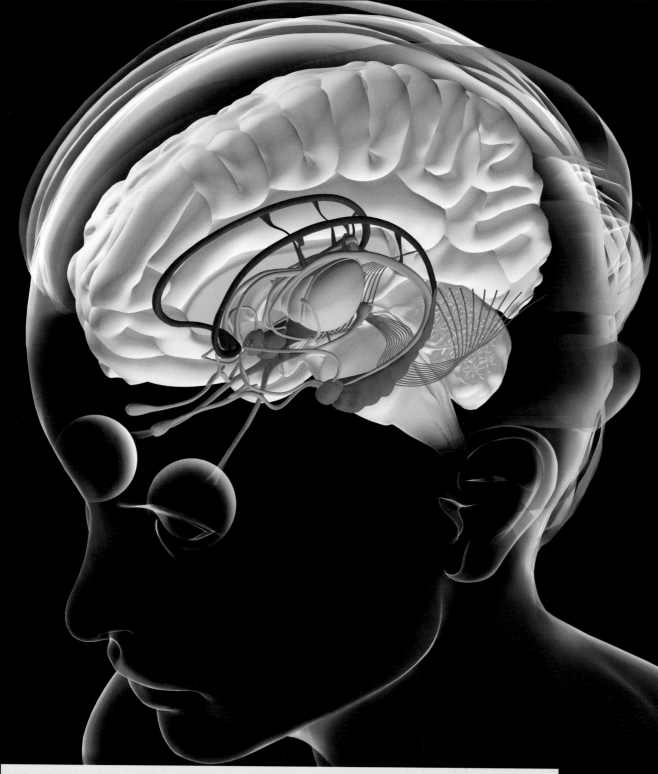

This picture shows parts of the brain, including the right hemisphere (light gray), the thalamus (blue), the hippocampus (purple), the amygdala (pink), the hypothalamus (dark blue), the olfactory bulbs (light green), and the optic nerves (orange). The visual cortex, also called visual area, is located at the very back of the brain. It is where visual information is organized into images that the brain can recognize.

inch (2.5 centimeters) away from your fingers under the skull bone and a layer of fluid.

The visual cortices break down the information collected from the eyes into its separate components, such as what colors, motion, and shapes are being observed. The secondary visual cortex then processes all of the data and identifies the objects in the field of vision, drawing upon prior memories and experiences.

For example, let's say you see someone who looks familiar to you across a crowded room, but you cannot quite place the face. Your eyes first spot the person and collect information about what he or she looks like. This information travels through the brain and ends up at the visual cortices. The secondary visual cortex compares the data with information already stored in your brain's memory. Sometimes when a match is made it feels like a light bulb is going off in your head. It is that moment when you finally remember who the person is.

Every waking moment, millions of nerve signals shoot through the brain and continually provide information about the people and the world around us. An almost magical feature of the visual cortices is that they allow us not only to see images in real time, but, because they store data to memory, they also enable us to re-create images, shapes, and colors in our imaginations. This way, we can create mental images of things we have viewed in the past. For example, when a friend or relative is away and you miss him or her, you can remember what the individual looks like because data about the person is stored in your brain.

CHAPTER THREE

THE VISUAL PROCESS

Your eyes discern light, and vision depends on the principles of light. Light is the medium by which information concerning the world around you is transmitted to your eyes. This concept sounds complicated, but really it is very simple. At some point, you have probably been in a room or closet that was so dark you could not see a thing. The objects in the room were still present even though they were not visible to you. If a flashlight had been turned on, only the areas near where the light shined would have been visible. That is because eyes pick up

Light enters the eye through the cornea and passes through the aqueous fluid, pupil, lens, and vitreous fluid and then reaches the retina. These structures help to refract, or bend, the light so it correctly focuses on the retina.

information based on the way light bounces off objects.

By itself, light travels in a straight line. But when light passes through certain materials, it can reflect and bend. In a dark room, try shining a flashlight in a mirror set at a right angle to a wall, such as a bathroom mirror. What do you see on the wall? The circle of light reflects onto the wall from the mirror, even though the light did not initially travel in that direction.

Because of their glasslike transparency and structure, the cornea and lens of the eye can bend light. Camera lenses have this ability, too, but often the lens has to be manually adjusted or changed to match the position of the object in the field of vision. The human eyes and muscles make such adjustments by themselves.

HOW YOUR EYES FORM IMAGES

Let's examine how, at this very second, your eyes are creating a visual image of this page. First, light reflected from the page hits the cornea. At this point the light entering your eye has already been condensed into manageable rays.

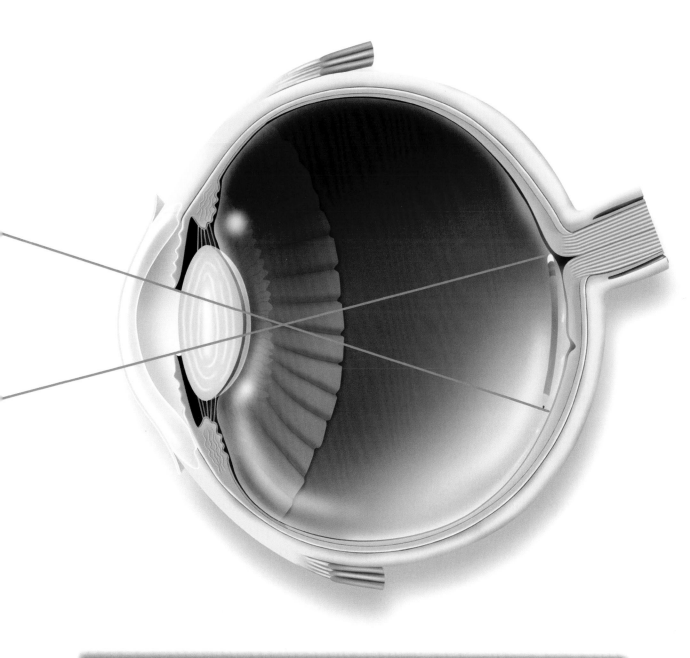

A reflected image such as this one of a pencil lands on the retina upside down. The brain interprets it and turns it right-side up. The lens is flexible, and the ciliary muscles that are attached to it can change its curved shape to focus on near or far objects.

Because light condenses information about objects and is able to bend, you can see the page even though it is much larger than your eyes. Televisions operate using a similar process.

Light bends when it hits the cornea and travels toward the iris. Ciliary muscles around the iris react to light in the room and cause the iris to open or close around the pupil. The muscles can cause the pupil to open anywhere from 1/25 of an inch (0.1 cm)—if light conditions are extremely bright—to 1/3 of an inch (0.8 cm) under darker conditions. Light travels through the pupil hole, where it reaches the lens.

Because it is likely that this page is close to your face, the lens identifies the page as a near object and the eye adjusts its focus accordingly. For near objects, eye muscles contract to make the lens short and round. If the page were far away, the eye muscles would cause the lens to become thin and long. These different shapes change the way the lens bends light. After passing through the lens, the light that initially bounced off the page reaches the light-sensing rod and cone cells on the retina at the back of the eye. Like a movie projector, the lens projects an image of the page on the retina. Surprisingly, the image is upside down!

This inverted image is what the optic nerve carries with it as nerve impulses send the image of the page to the brain's optic chiasma, the lateral geniculate body, the optic radiation, the internal capsule, and finally to the primary and secondary visual cortices. The page does not appear to be upside down because the brain transposes the image to match what the brain thinks it should be seeing. Humans are not born with this skill. It has to be learned. Newborn babies, for example, can see, but they have

DECEIVING THE EYES: OPTICAL ILLUSIONS

Optical illusions are visual tricks that fool the brain. Because the brain must interpret, or process, information collected in the eyes, it learns to react to certain patterns. When these patterns are broken, the brain still functions as it normally would, and an optical illusion may result.

Try this trick. Roll a sheet of paper into a tube. Hold the tube up to your right eye with your right hand while holding your left hand, palm facing forward, at the side end of the tube. Gradually bring your left hand toward your face, running it alongside the tube. The brain registers that you have a hole in your left hand!

An optical illusion makes the pinwheels in this moiré pattern look like they are turning. Certain patterns, colors, and light can make images that mislead your brain and create captivating visual effects.

no sense of direction. Over a short period of time they learn to associate the position of objects in relation to other things and soon see right-side-up.

After the brain has finished processing the now right-side-up object in the visual cortex region, the mind creates an instantaneous mental image of the page and stores this image away in memory. Because memory can last for many years, the image of this page, and the information gleaned from it, may last in your memory well into the future.

3D PERCEPTION PRODUCED BY TWO FIELDS OF VISION

If you had one big eye in the middle of your forehead, it would not only look rather odd, but you would also not have very good depth perception, or the ability to gauge the distance from one object to another. Two eyes allow people to see everything in 3D, or three dimensions. This ability is called stereoscopic vision.

Stereoscopic vision is possible because each eye has a slightly different field of vision. The brain combines the two images into one when the two optic nerves leading from each eye send impulses down the nerve pathways toward the visual cortex region. Although the images captured in the left and right eyes are combined and processed by the brain, people still retain information about what was seen by each individual eye.

CORRECTIVE LENSES CALLED CONTACT LENSES

Unlike eyeglasses, which are worn on the face, contact lenses are inserted directly over the cornea. Contacts have certain advantages and disadvantages. On the plus side, contacts provide good peripheral, or side, vision. They stay in place during high impact activities, such as sports, and they provide a nearly invisible way to correct nearsightedness, farsightedness, and astigmatism.

Contacts, however, require more maintenance than eyeglasses and must be kept clean at all times. Some individuals also find them uncomfortable to wear. If you need corrective lenses, your optometrist should provide advice and information about obtaining either eyeglasses or contacts.

Contact lenses correct vision and can be worn instead of eyeglasses. Sometimes they are designed to change the color of the natural iris.

In sports, sometimes people will try to improve their ability to judge distance. Many golfers, for example, will try to determine a ball's distance and direction from the hole by squatting on the ground, to provide a more level field of vision, or by closing one eye to devote their

In stereoscopic vision, two distinct views of an object taken by the eyes from slightly different angles are successfully interpreted as one image in the brain. The object is viewed in three dimensions (width, height, and depth). In this picture, the left eye sees a bit more of the left side of the butterfly, while the right sees more of the right side. Your brain interprets the information, and the angle that your eyes have to turn to focus on the butterfly, to give you an estimate of the butterfly's distance from you.

attention to a single area. Target shooters, pool players, and dart players will also often close one eye to improve direct focus on a single target and to eliminate some of the 3D effects of stereoscopic vision.

COLOR PERCEPTION

Cone cells in the retina enable humans to detect three basic colors in light: red, green, and blue. Each of these three colors stimulates a slightly different type of cone cell. Variations in the intensity of these colors and the processing performed by the brain give us the ability to detect a full rainbow spectrum of colors.

Each cone cell contains 100 million molecules of a substance called a photopigment. These retinal molecules chemically change in the presence of light because all light contains a certain amount of energy. For example, think of how light from the sun can produce solar energy. When struck by light, a retinal molecule twists around, which causes other chemical reactions to take place inside the cone. The cone then generates a nerve impulse that travels through the optic nerve to the brain, which registers the observed color. Incredibly, this multistep process occurs many millions of times each second in each of the eye's cone cells.

Sometimes, colors in bright light can leave a lasting image on the retina. You may have experienced this after having your picture taken with a camera that uses a flash. When this happens, the round light

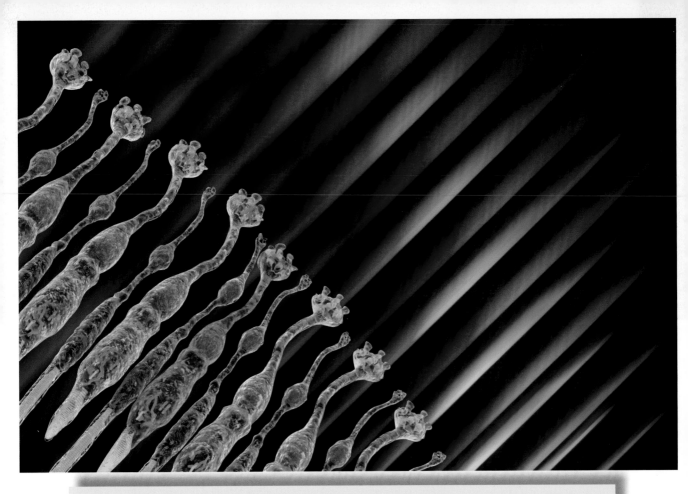

Pictured here are rods and cones, the photoreceptors of the retina. Cones have the large flower-like endings. Rods detect the light and dark tones in images but do not help in discerning color. The cones assist in perceiving lines, points, and colors, and are not as sensitive to light as rods. The colors above the rods and cones represent light coming through the iris.

of the flash remains in your field of vision for a few seconds after the picture was snapped. The light-sensing cells of the retina become over-stimulated. Staring at direct sunlight and other bright objects can also over-stimulate cells in the eye and may cause permanent damage.

CHAPTER FOUR

EYE PROBLEMS AND VISUAL DISORDERS

Good vision necessitates that all of the diverse parts and systems required for sight are functioning correctly. Optometrists and ophthalmologists check to make sure that the cornea and lens focus properly. They check the eyes' sensitivity to different light levels. They also measure the pressure of fluid within the eyeballs. An optometrist is a health care professional who is a licensed nonmedical doctor of optometry and who is trained to deal with the functioning of the eyes but not the diseases of the eyes. He or she measures refraction and prescribes and fits eyeglasses or contact lenses. An ophthalmologist is a physician who specializes in diagnosing and treating disorders and diseases of the eyes. He or she performs surgery when required and can prescribe other treatment, including eyeglasses and contacts.

Eye charts allow optometrists and ophthalmologists to determine how well you can see both up close and at a distance.

Ophthalmologists and optometrists test people's sharpness of vision to perceive detail by measuring their ability to read letters and numbers on a chart, sometimes called a Snellen chart, from a specific distance.

Letters or numbers on the chart usually begin large and get smaller and smaller. Individuals who can see clearly at the prescribed distance of 20 feet (6 meters), and do not experience eyestrain, are said to have 20/20 vision, or normal eyesight. Visual acuity, the clearness or sharpness of vision, depends on retinal focus within the eye. Visual acuity measurement for a person with normal vision, therefore, is 20/20. A person with 20/70 vision, for example, who is 20 feet (6 m) away from an eye chart observes what an individual with 20/20 vision can see from 70 feet (21 m) away. The person with 20/70 might be said to have low vision.

Just as with a car or computer with many sophisticated parts, problems can affect one or more parts of the body involved in sight. Sometimes these problems come at birth, with structural faults in the eyeball or lens. Age is also a factor. Just as a car or computer can develop problems over time, so, too, can the eyes. Certain parts simply wear out and need to be treated or replaced. By far the most common visual defects are nearsightedness and farsightedness, with about thirty-four million Americans who are forty years old or older having nearsightedness and nearly fourteen million Americans age forty and older having farsightedness, according to preventblindness.org.

MYOPIA OR NEARSIGHTEDNESS

Myopia, or nearsightedness, occurs when a person has long eyeballs or lenses that refract too much. Refraction refers to the bending of light. Nearsighted individuals can see objects that are close to them but have trouble distinguishing objects that are far away. For example, a nearsighted person standing in front of a classroom or an auditorium may be able to clearly see the first few rows of people, but the rest of the room looks like a fuzzy blur.

Good vision requires that the focal point, or the place where light waves converge in the eye, hits the retina. The light rays enter the eye in a V shape, with the open part of the V corresponding to the top and bottom of an object. In a person with 20/20 vision,

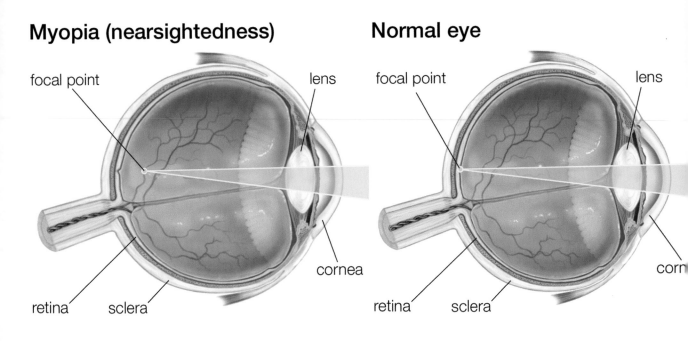

Myopia (nearsightedness)

focal point
lens
retina
sclera
cornea

Normal eye

focal point
lens
retina
sclera
corn

The focal points in myopia (left) and a normal eye are compared here. The myopic, or nearsighted, eye is elongated, and its focal point falls short of the back of the retina. A concave lens can be used to correct the refractive error.

the pointy V convergence usually lands right on the fovea, where most of the eye's rod and cone cells are located. In a person with nearsightedness, the convergence, or the point of perfect focus, occurs in front of the retina.

Nearsightedness is easily cleared up with corrective lenses, meaning glasses or contact lenses. The corrective lens for myopia is concave, or hollow and curved inward, like the inside of a bowl. The concave lens extends the light wave convergence in the eye to the retina.

RETINAL DETACHMENTS

A common condition that affects people who are nearsighted is retinal detachment. This condition usually occurs in individuals who are age sixty and older, but it can happen at any age and actually with any refractive situation. Retinal detachments frequently result from a problem with the vitreous that causes shrinkage of

(continued on the next page)

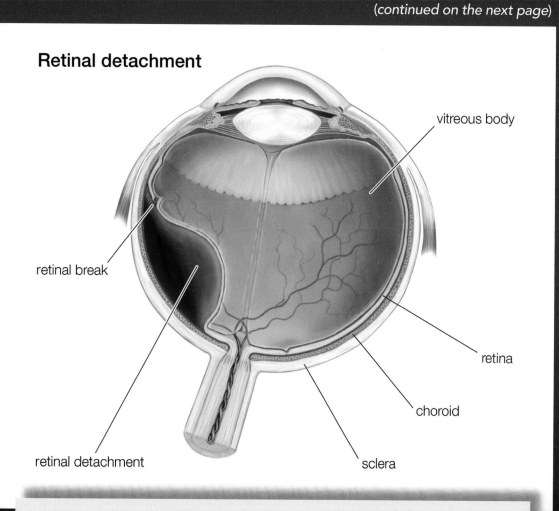

Retinal detachment

vitreous body

retinal break

retinal detachment

sclera

choroid

retina

A retinal detachment can be caused by a number of factors, including the vitreous shrinking and pulling away from the retina. Retinal breaks or tears can allow vitreous fluid to get behind the retina and pull it off.

(continued from the previous page)

the fluid, which fills the center of the eyeball and assists in holding the retina in place next to the choroid. If the vitreous contracts and pulls away from the retina, it can cause a tear in the retina. There are other causes for retinal tears, such as an eye injury, including bruising or being hit on the head, or having other health conditions. If the retina breaks away from the choroid, the vitreous fluid often slips behind the retina and can cause it to detach, or separate, or to tear even more. If this situation is left untreated, the detached retina will not be able to receive its nutrients and will no longer function.

Certain procedures allow an eye surgeon to repair a retinal detachment or reduce the chance of further detachment, including using lasers to seal the tears. One procedure is called scleral indenting or buckling, which decreases the circumference of the eyeball and pushes the scleral wall against the retina. An eye surgeon places a scleral buckle on the outside of the eye, which helps to push in the sclera toward the center of the eye. This buckle effect relieves the pulling on the retina and helps the tear to lie against the wall of the eye. Yet another surgical operation, called a vitrectomy, removes the vitreous fluid and can include treatment of the retina with a laser. Near the end of this surgery, a gas bubble or silicone oil is injected into the eyeball to help press the retina against the wall of the eye. The gas bubble is gradually absorbed by the body; however, if oil is used, there must be a second operation to remove it, because oil cannot be absorbed by the body. The goal is to reattach the retina so it receives its nutrients and improves vision.

HYPEROPIA OR FARSIGHTEDNESS

Hyperopia, or farsightedness, allows affected individuals to view objects clearly that are far away, but nearby objects appear blurred. Weak lenses that cannot produce enough refraction or eyeballs that are too short in shape are the cause. The eyeball of a farsighted person looks a bit like an egg standing upright while the eyeball of a nearsighted person looks more like an egg resting on its side.

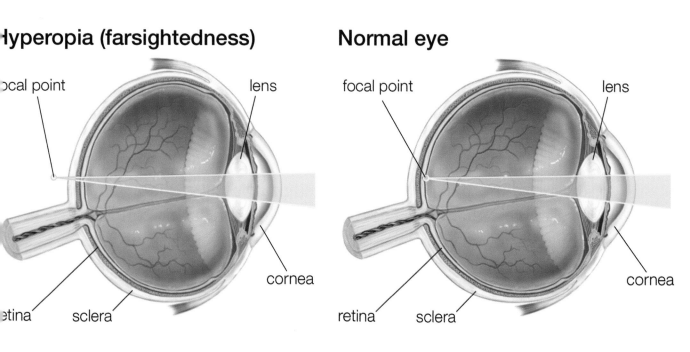

The focal point of a hyperopic, or farsighted, eye (left) is compared with that of a normal eye. In hyperopia, where the eye is usually shorter than a normal eye, the light rays converge behind the retina. This refractive error can be corrected by using a convex lens.

Light convergence in the eyes of a farsighted person falls past the retina. The pointy end of the V goes past the eye. Wearing convex corrective lenses can solve this problem. Convex means to curve outward. The disklike shape enables the individual to focus light rays onto the retina.

THE VISION CONDITION CALLED ASTIGMATISM

Another eye problem that can be corrected by wearing either eyeglasses or contact lenses is called astigmatism. A person with this condition may have an irregularly curved cornea or an irregularity in the shape of the eyeball. Instead of the eye being a round shape, the eye with astigmatism can a shape similar to a football. With astigmatism, rays of light entering the eye bend in different ways. Some are focused correctly, while others may bend too much. This causes distortion of viewed objects. For example, the person may see a slightly blurry double image of an object that otherwise appears clear. With this condition, objects viewed at all distances can be affected. Individuals with astigmatism often complain of getting headaches from straining the eyes while reading or watching TV.

Astigmatism is corrected by wearing cylindrical lenses, which look a bit like tubes that have been sliced in half. This shape helps to bend light inward to create a proper focus of light convergence on the retina.

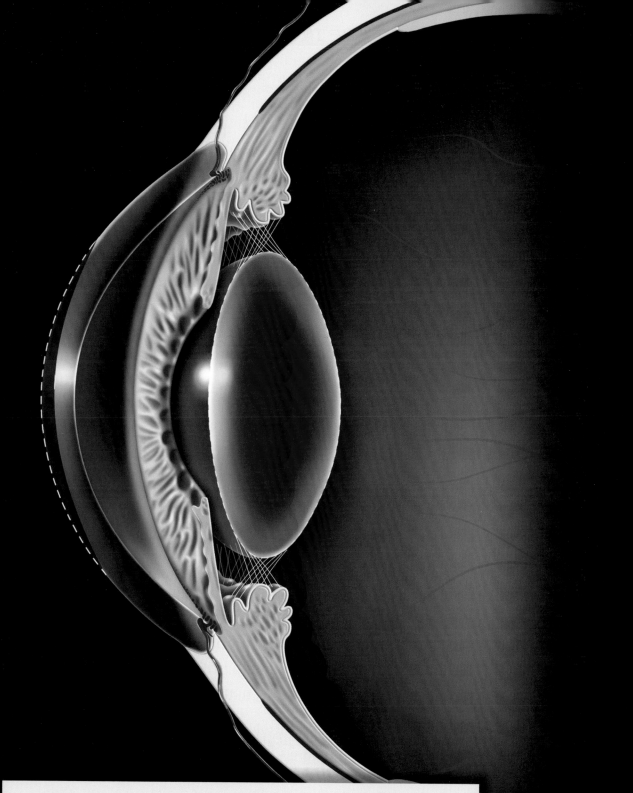

In astigmatism, the cornea is often oval-shaped instead of spherical. Astigmatism can occur in people who are nearsighted and farsighted. To correct this type of refractive error, a cylindrical lens, sometimes called a Toric lens, is used.

THE COLOR VISION PROBLEM CALLED COLOR BLINDNESS

Though rare in females, approximately 8 percent of males inherit a condition known as color blindness. People with this condition are missing one or more types of cones for a certain color group. Red-green color blindness is most common and prevents the person from distinguishing between red and green. Usually the problem is not very serious, because most shades of red are not pure and have a bit of yellow in them, and most greens contain some blue. Therefore color-blind people who drive generally do not have difficulties seeing changing traffic lights.

AN INCREASE IN EYE PRESSURE: GLAUCOMA

Other, more serious diseases can affect the eye and may cause permanent damage. Glaucoma, for example, is a disease that disrupts the flow of the aqueous humor in front of the iris and pupil. The change in flow may then cause pressure to build up in the entire eye. That is why eye doctors usually measure your eye pressure.

If the disease is identified early, medication or surgery can restore proper aqueous humor flow. If the disease is left untreated, the high pressure can destroy cells in the retina and

This photograph represents what people who have glaucoma or retinitis pigmentosa (a disease characterized by decreasing peripheral vision) might see in their visual field as their conditions progress. If they are not treated, the result could be total blindness.

cause vision loss or blindness. Certain individuals can be pre-disposed to developing glaucoma because of genetic factors or complications from diabetes or high blood pressure.

CLOUDING OF THE LENSES: CATARACTS

Over time, cells in the lens of the eye can lose their transparency and cloud up, like a window covered with a white film. The cloudy, opaque areas are called cataracts. Although the condition is painless, it can cause blurred vision and difficulty in distinguishing colors. Surgery usually corrects the problem. Doctors can remove the affected lens and can either replace it with a new one or restore the lost vision with corrective lenses.

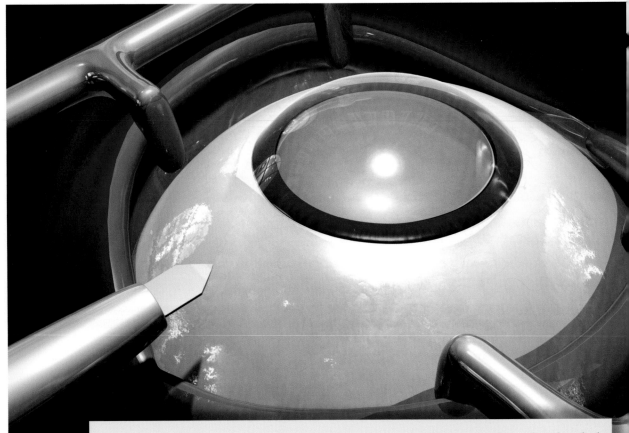

This image shows an eye with a cataract during surgery to replace the clouded lens with a lens implant. A surgeon uses retractors to hold the iris away from the lens and a scalpel to make the first cut to extract the damaged lens.

LOSS OF CENTRAL VISION: MACULAR DEGENERATION

As the human life span continues to increase, so, too, does the risk of developing macular degeneration. When a person gets older, blood flow to the eye may decrease, causing a lack of oxygen and nutrients in the retina. Rods and cones in the macula or fovea are especially sensitive to such changes and can gradually deteriorate, causing loss of vision.

THE INABILITY TO SEE: BLINDNESS

Blindness, or complete vision loss, can occur at birth or as a result of an illness or accident. The damage or defect may be in the eyes or the brain region. But because the brain is involved in the vision process and is highly adaptable, blind individuals can compensate for the loss of vision with other senses, such as hearing and touch. Many blind people, for example, read using a special raised alphabet known as Braille. Patterns of dots coinciding with letters can be felt with the fingertips. Guide dogs can also help blind individuals to lead more independent lives. The dogs are trained to be the eyes of the owners, thus enabling people to navigate safely outdoors and in unfamiliar places.

GLOSSARY

AQUEOUS HUMOR Fluid located between the cornea and lens that nourishes and protects the eye. It also helps to maintain proper pressure within the eyeball.

ASTIGMATISM Condition caused by an irregularly curved cornea or an irregularity in the shape of the eyeball. Astigmatism distorts images, making them seem blurry or doubled.

BLIND SPOT The place where the optic nerve leaves the eye. Because this small region of the eye does not contain any rods or cones, it creates a blind area in our fields of vision. Since the brain makes up for the missing view, we do not usually notice the blind spot.

CILIARY MUSCLES Small, stringlike muscles that change the shape of the lens and help to open and close the iris.

CIRCUMFERENCE The outer edge of a curved geometric figure such as a circle or globe.

CONES Light-sensing cells within the retina that allow us to see color.

CONJUNCTIVA Transparent, protective outer first layer of the eye.

CONVERGENCE Coming together from different directions and joining.

CORNEA A clear, five-layered disk at the front of the eye that helps with focusing. It does 75 percent of the eye's work.

CORRECTIVE LENSES Eyeglasses or contact lenses that can correct eye problems, such as astigmatism, nearsightedness, and farsightedness, by changing the way that the eye bends and focuses light.

CRYSTALLINE Transparent, very clear, or like a crystal.

DIGITAL Having to do with the use of computer technology. A digital camera does not use film to take pictures, but instead uses digital data to record images.

FARSIGHTEDNESS A condition, commonly caused by eyeballs that are too short or lenses that are too weak, that keeps affected individuals from clearly seeing nearby objects. They can, however, see objects at a distance.

FOVEA An indentation in the center of the macula.

GLAUCOMA A disease in which increasing eye pressure causes damage to the optic disk and eventually affects the visual field. If left untreated, glaucoma can result in blindness.

IRIS The colored part of the eye that controls how much light can enter through the pupil.

LENS Transparent, flexible disk located behind the pupil that focuses light, a process begun by the cornea.

MACULA The part of the retina containing the most rod and cone cells. Light that converges here produces the clearest images.

MELANIN Substance that gives color to the iris, skin, and hair.

NEARSIGHTEDNESS A condition, commonly caused by eyeballs that are too long or lenses that refract too much, that prohibits affected individuals from clearly seeing objects that are far away.

OPTIC CHIASMA Place in the brain where the optic nerves from each eye meet to exchange information.

OPTIC NERVE A nerve that runs from the retina of each eye. It carries information gathered by the eye's light-sensing cells through the brain.

OPTOMETRY The profession or practice of giving eye examinations to determine visual disorders and defects and to prescribe corrective lenses.

PIXEL An abbreviation for "picture element," a pixel is one point or unit in a graphic image. Each digital photograph is made up of pixels.

PRESCRIBE To tell someone formally that he or she needs to use a medicine or other type of treatment.

PUPIL Hole through which light enters the eye.

REFRACTION The bending of light; determining the refractive errors of the eyes, such as nearsightedness and farsightedness, and their correction with eyeglasses or contact lenses.

RETINA The part at the back of the eye that contains light-sensing cells that enable us to interpret images from light reflected off of objects.

RETINAL DETACHMENT The separation of the retina from the choroid, usually caused by a retinal tear. Surgery generally has to be performed to prevent the loss of vision.

RODS Light-sensing cells in the retina that define clear, sharp images, even in low light. They are named for their shape.

SCLERA Tough, white part of the eye.

SENSORY Having to do with the senses; sensory nerves carry nerve impulses from the organs of the senses to the brain.

TEARS Protective fluid, made in the lacrimal glands just above the eyes and released through the inside of the upper eyelids, that helps to protect the eyes from dust, germs, and other things that could cause damage.

THALAMUS A part of the forebrain that is located above the brain stem and receives nerve signals and relays them to other parts of the brain cortex.

20/20 VISION Term used to describe individuals with normal vision who can, without eyestrain, clearly see at the prescribed distance of 20 feet (6 meters).

VISUAL CORTEX The rear portion of the brain that processes visual information supplied by the optic nerve.

VITREOUS HUMOR Thick, jellylike fluid located in the main chamber of each eye, behind the lens, that gives the eyes their rubbery texture.

FOR MORE INFORMATION

American Academy of Ophthalmology

P.O. Box 7424

San Francisco, CA 94120-7424

(415) 561-8500

Website: http://www.aao.org

This association of eye medical doctors provides support and learning programs for its members. Its website offers information about eye diseases and conditions, eyeglasses, contacts, and LASIK procedures; finding doctors in your region; and consumer alerts.

American Diabetes Association

1701 North Beauregard Street

Alexandria, VA 22311

(800) 342-2383

Website: http://www.diabetes.org

This association works to help people who have diabetes manage their condition. It offers several online resources, including tips on living with diabetes, meal planning, and recipes, and it delivers services to communities and funds research to cure diabetes. Its website contains information on eye complications caused by diabetes.

American Foundation for the Blind (AFB)

2 Penn Plaza, Suite 1102

New York, NY 10121

(212) 502-7600

Website: http://www.afb.org

AFB helps people with visual impairment to obtain equal access and reach their full potential through educational programs and advocacy.

American Optometric Association (AOA)

243 North Lindbergh Boulevard, Floor 1

St. Louis, MO 63141-7881

(800) 365-2219

Website: http://www.aoa.org

The AOA represents students and doctors of optometry and helps them in providing vision care to the public.

The Association for Macular Diseases, Inc.

210 East 64th Street

New York, NY 10065

Hotline: (212) 605-3719

Website: http://macula.org

This association provides information and assistance to people with macular disease and their caregivers.

Canadian Council of the Blind (CCB)

20 James Street, Suite 100

Ottawa, ON K2P 0T6

Canada

(613) 567-0311

Website: http://www.ccbnational.net

The CCB provides social, recreational, and blindness prevention programs for people who are blind or have vision disorders.

Eye Foundation of Canada

2115 Finch Avenue, Suite 314

Toronto, ON M3N 2V6

Canada

(416) 743-9046

Website: http://eyefoundationcanada.ca

This not-for-profit organization works to provide quality eye care for all Canadians. It also offers a scholarship program for medical students who are starting their careers.

Foundation Fighting Blindness

7168 Columbia Gateway Drive, Suite 100

Columbia, SC 21046

(800) 683-5555

Website: http://www.blindness.org

The foundation's mission is to encourage research to prevent, treat, and cure blinding retinal disorders.

Glaucoma Research Foundation

251 Post Street, Suite 600

San Francisco, CA 94108

(800) 826-6693

Website: http://www.glaucoma.org

This nonprofit organization works to find a cure for glaucoma. It supports glaucoma research around the world.

Lighthouse International

111 East 59th Street

New York, NY 10022-1202

(800) 284-4422

Website: http://www.lighthouse.org

This organization works to prevent vision loss and treat people who have visual impairments. Its website also provides products for sale that help people who have eye disorders.

National Eye Institute (NEI)

31 Center Drive

Bethesda, MD 20892-2510

(301) 496-5248

Website: http://www.nei.nih.gov

This agency is part of the U.S. government's National Institutes of Health. It conducts and encourages research on eye diseases and provides health information about vision and visual disorders to the public.

Prevent Blindness America

211 West Wacker Drive, Suite 1700

Chicago, IL 60606

(800) 331-2020

Website: http://www.preventblindness.org

This volunteer eye health and safety organization works to prevent blindness and save people's sight. It supports routine vision care and educates the public about eye health.

WEBSITES

Because of the changing nature of Internet links, Rosen Publishing has developed an online list of websites related to the subject of this book. This site is updated regularly. Please use this link to access the list:

http://www.rosenlinks.com/HB3D/Eye

FOR FURTHER READING

Alcamo, I. Edward, and Barbara Krumhardt. *E-Z Anatomy and Physiology* (Barron's E-Z Series). Hauppauge, NY: Barron's Educational Services, 2010.

Ashwell, Ken W. S. *The Brain Book: Development, Function, Disorder, Health*. Buffalo, NY: Firefly Books, 2012.

Baars, Paul. *Optical Illusions*. New York, NY: Abrams, 2013.

Brynie, Faith Hickman. *Brain Sense: The Science of the Senses and How We Process the World Around Us*. New York, NY: American Management Association, 2009.

Gillard, Arthur, ed. *Traumatic Brain Injury* (Perspectives on Diseases and Disorders). Detroit, MI: Greenhaven Press, 2014.

Green, Leslie C. *I Have Diabetes. Now What?* New York, NY: Rosen Publishing, 2012.

Horstman, Judith. *The Scientific American Day in the Life of Your Brain*. San Francisco, CA: Jossey-Bass, 2009.

Jackson, Donna M. *Phenomena: Secrets of the Senses*. New York, NY: Little, Brown and Co., 2008.

Jenkins, Steve. *Eye to Eye: How Animals See the World*. Boston, MA: Houghton Mifflin Harcourt, 2014.

Lang, Susan. *Senses, Nervous System & Respiratory System* (Human Body Series). San Diego, CA: Classroom Complete Press, 2007.

Livingstone, Margaret, and David H. Hubel. *Vision and Art: The Biology of Seeing*. Revised and expanded ed. New York, NY: Abrams, 2014.

Mooney, Carla. *Brain: Journey Through the Universe Inside Your Head*. White River Junction, VT: Nomad Press, 2015.

Rogers, Kara, ed. *Bone and Muscle: Structure, Force, and Motion* (The Human Body). New York, NY: Britannica Educational Publishing, 2011.

Rogers, Kara, ed. *The Eye: The Physiology of Human Perception* (The Human Body). New York, NY: Britannica Educational Publishing, 2011.

Silverstein, Alvin, Virginia B. Silverstein, and Laura Silverstein Nunn. *Handy Health Guide to Your Eyes*. Berkeley Heights, NJ: Enslow Publishers, 2014.

Snedden, Robert. *Understanding the Brain and the Nervous System* (Understanding the Human Body). New York, NY: Rosen Publishing, 2010.

Stamps, Caroline. *Human Body* (Eyewonder). New York, NY: DK Publishing, 2013.

Stimola, Aubrey. *Brain Injuries* (Understanding Brain Diseases and Disorders). New York, NY: Rosen Publishing, 2012.

Sutton, Amy L. *Eye Care Sourcebook* (Health Reference Series). 3rd ed. Detroit, MI: Omnigraphics, 2008.

Walker, Richard. *Eyewitness: The Human Body*. New York, NY: DK Publishing, 2009.

INDEX

ABOUT THE AUTHORS

Rusty Huddle is a writer who has myopia (nearsightedness) and has had three surgeries for detached retinas and two vitrectomies (the surgical removal of the vitreous humor). He lives in Westchester County, New York.

Jennifer Viegas, a nearsighted writer who wears contacts, is a reporter for Discovery News. She has worked as a journalist for ABC News, PBS, the *Washington Post*, the *Christian Science Monitor*, and several other publications, and focuses on subjects related to science. Viegas is based in San Francisco, California.

PHOTO CREDITS

Designer: Brian Garvey; Editor: Kathy Kuhtz Campbell; Photo Researcher: Karen Huang